D0843126

Dr. Josef Mengele
The Angel of Death

Holly Cefrey

THE ROSEN PUBLISHING GROUP, INC.
NEW YORK

Published in 2001 by The Rosen Publishing Group, Inc.
29 East 21st Street, New York, NY 10010

First Edition

Library of Congress Cataloging-in-Publication Data

Cefrey, Holly.
Dr. Josef Mengele : the angel of death / by Holly Cefrey.
p. cm. — (Holocaust biographies)
Includes bibliographical references and index.
ISBN 0-8239-3374-1
1. Mengele, Josef, 1911——Juvenile literature. 2. War
criminals—Germany—Biography—Juvenile literature.
3. World War, 1939–1945—Atrocities—Juvenile literature.
4. Germany—Social conditions—1933–1945—Juvenile
literature. 5. Physicians—Germany—Biography—Juvenile
literature. [1. Mengele, Josef, 1911– 2. War criminals—
Germany. 3. World War, 1939–1945—Atrocities. 4. Germany—
Social conditions—1933–1945. 5. Physicians.] I. Title.
II. Series.
DD247.M46 C44 2001
364.15'1'092—dc21

2001001655

Manufactured in the United States of America

Contents

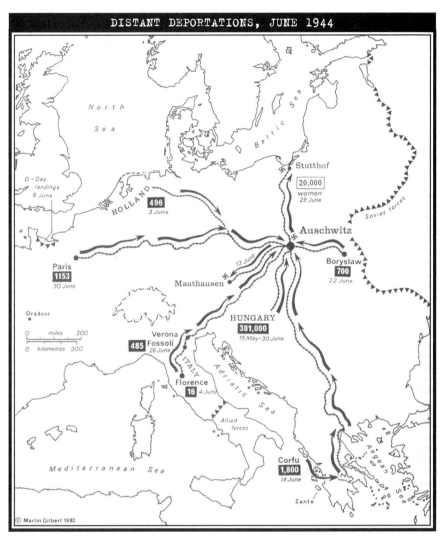

DISTANT DEPORTATIONS, JUNE 1944

Deportations to Auschwitz continued even as World War II was drawing to a close. Trains of prisoners reached Auschwitz from throughout occupied Europe. The numbers on the map reflect the numbers of prisoners transported to Auschwitz during May and June of 1944.

Introduction

They arrived by the thousands: Jews, Catholics, Gypsies, and Jehovah's Witnesses; Soviet, Polish, and German prisoners of war; and the physically and mentally challenged. After spending days on a train—not a passenger train but a cattle car meant for livestock—they arrived. They didn't come to this place for vacation, work, or school. They were brought here against their will, to be murdered.

Before the exhausting journey, many of the Jews had struggled to survive in the ghettos. All of their belongings were taken from them, but they remembered how, months before, they had been in school, run businesses, or played outdoor games with friends and family. They had lived normal lives. All of them had names, but in the camps, these, too, were taken from them. In place of their birth names, many of them were given numbers, which were tattooed onto their arms. Along with the numbers came the harsh reality that they now belonged to Germany and its Third Reich.

If you had been with them in this cattle car, you would have seen how their last days were spent. They were crammed into the trains without food or drink. In order to relieve themselves, they had to use a single bucket. Some trains didn't have buckets—or even blankets—just the hard floor beneath. Many people died on the trains. On several trips, the bodies were not removed until the train reached its final destination. Imagine being herded into a cramped, filthy space. Imagine that next to you is the body of a loved one who has just died. It's a horrifying thought, but it was reality for millions of innocent prisoners— mostly Jews—during World War II.

This true story of torture doesn't end with the train trip. When the train met its destination, German soldiers were waiting outside with guns. They ordered the prisoners out with aggressive shouting. The prisoners were tired, starving, and confused. Some of the prisoners already knew of this place—they had received postcards from relatives who had been sent here. Little did they know that the postcards had been falsely written, and that their relatives were most likely dead. Little did they know that they had been brought to the Third Reich's largest death camp, Auschwitz.

The German soldiers roughly guided hundreds of prisoners out onto the railway platform. Whatever valuables the prisoners had been allowed to bring were now hurriedly left behind. The prisoners were instructed to form two lines, one for men and one for women. They were about to undergo one of the most haunting ordeals of the Holocaust— the *Selektionen*. This was the process by which the Nazis—headed by Nazi doctors—decided who would become a slave in the labor camp and who would be murdered immediately.

Prisoners were instructed by a *Selektionen* doctor to go either to the right or left. Going to the right meant that they would join the labor camp where they would be worked to death. Going to the left meant that this would be their last day on Earth. Those sent to their deaths were deemed unfit for slave work. Most children, elderly, disabled people, and pregnant women were immediately sent to die. Those

This warehouse is full of the shoes and clothing that the Nazis confiscated from the prisoners. The goods were eventually shipped to Germany.

sent to the left did not know that they would be dead in less than an hour. They were led to believe that they needed to take showers before entering the labor camp.

They were marched in long lines to the shower buildings. Electrified fences surrounded the walkway to the showers. Some prisoners, sensing doom, threw themselves on the fences and committed suicide. Once in the locked shower unit, a toxic gas was released and the prisoners painfully choked to death on the fumes. More than one hundred prisoners were murdered during each gassing. These mass murders took place several times a day.

◆ ◆ ◆

The prisoners who survived Auschwitz remember a German soldier and doctor who took pleasure in leading the selection process. His name was Dr. Josef Mengele and he was known as the Angel of Death. His personality was a combination of pleasantness and perversity. He stood on the railway platform in an impeccable uniform with white gloves. He

The body of a prisoner who committed suicide by throwing himself on an electrified barbed wire fence.

often had a cheerful expression on his face, and was heard humming classical music by many prisoners. He wore perfectly polished boots and held a riding crop. Many times his pleasant demeanor would turn wicked, and he would beat prisoners with his crop while shouting at them. He would often send otherwise healthy prisoners to their deaths because they had skin blemishes or minor imperfections.

Mengele's eyes would widen in excitement whenever he encountered twins at the *Selektionen*. He, like many other Nazi doctors, used the prisoners for experimentation. He was especially interested in twins. Nazi doctors knew that the prisoners were going to die anyway, so prisoners were used for numerous deadly experiments. Most of the experiments were of little or no value to medical science, and most were cruel and barbaric. These men called themselves doctors, but instead of healing the sick, they caused the suffering, disease, torture, and deaths of millions of innocent human beings.

1. Young Mengele

Josef Mengele was capable of great emotional and mental extremes. He was a doctor of known academic intelligence, yet he was able to take pleasure in a senseless process that led millions of victims to their deaths. He was cruel toward most of the Jews and other prisoners, but gentler toward the hundreds of twins and others that he used as research subjects at Auschwitz. Many of the twins and Gypsy children of the camp even referred to him as Uncle Pepi. His gentleness could end abruptly, though. He personally led some of the children to their deaths in the gas chamber.

Many Auschwitz survivors witnessed and remember his contradictions. He was a cultivated, good-looking man, yet during a moment of anger he could become a savage. This man of contradictions was more than a doctor gone wrong. He was part of a whole system that had gone wrong. He was a man following a demented system of beliefs that were deeply rooted in his upbringing. These beliefs were supported by many parts of German society and government. As a youth, he was exposed to these corrupt beliefs. He would later use them to justify his own actions as a murderous doctor.

Josef Mengele's beliefs allowed him to use humans as guinea pigs and to send many people to their deaths, without feeling remorse or shame. His beliefs allowed him to behave more like a monster than a doctor. He never faltered in his wrongheaded belief that he and the Nazi organization were doing what was right for the German people. To him, the crimes and injustices that the Nazis committed were necessary for the welfare of Germany and, ultimately, for the good of Europe as a whole.

The German Welfare

Josef Mengele was born in Germany on March 16, 1911. This was three years before World War I. The war took place mostly in Europe and involved many of the world's most powerful countries. The events that took place before and after World War I played a major role in shaping the lives of many Germans, including Mengele. Many historians believe that one of the causes of the war was that each country involved had its own strong sense of nationalism.

Nationalism is a political philosophy or belief that the welfare of one's nation is the most important thing. In this definition, the word "nation" means any community or culture with its own territory and government. The sense of nationalism in a country is strengthened if the people of that country share common characteristics. These characteristics can include ethnic background, religion, language, history, and moral beliefs.

Each country can have its own idea of what is best for its welfare. A country's nationalist beliefs are established and enforced on many levels. Adults and rulers establish nationalist beliefs through a government or ruling unit. Children and teens are taught nationalist beliefs in school, church, youth groups, the family, and through the media. Josef Mengele was born at a time when Germany's sense of nationalism was very strong. The German Empire promoted the belief that Germany could be the pre-eminent power in Europe, and even the world. This belief led Germany into World War I.

Austria-Hungary started the war on July 28, 1914, motivated by nationalist concerns. Germany decided to support Austria-Hungary in the war. In a military maneuver on August 2, 1914, Germany sought to attack France by way of Belgium. Belgium was neutral—that is, it took no active part in the war—and would not permit German troops to travel across its territory. Not willing to back down, Germany decided to cross Belgium by force. The following day, Great Britain declared war on Germany for its act against Belgium.

The war lasted longer than anyone could have imagined, and it devastated many areas of Europe. On October 4, 1918, Germany asked for terms of a truce. Due to the changes of war, the empires of Europe were overthrown and replaced by new governments. The German Empire, led by the Kaiser, was replaced with a new German government called the Weimar Republic. In answer to Germany's request for a truce, the Allies created the Versailles Treaty.

The treaty demanded that Germany accept full responsibility for the war. The treaty placed many restrictions on Germany. Germany was forced to let go of territories, colonies, and large military groups. Germany was asked to make payments for war damages in excess of 132 billion gold marks, or about 31 billion dollars. The leaders of the Weimar Republic

World leaders, including U.S. president Woodrow Wilson,
sign the Treaty of Versailles on June 28, 1919.

accepted the conditions of the treaty. This acceptance humiliated many nationalist Germans, who felt that Germany was superior and had been cheated of victory.

During the following years, Germany faced a deep economic depression. Many Germans blamed the loss of the war and the resulting financial depression on the liberal leaders of the Weimar Republic. Many of the liberals were

Jewish. Soon, many Nationalist Germans were saying that the liberal Jews had tricked Germany into accepting the treaty in order to weaken the German state. Some Germans also suggested that the Versailles Treaty must be broken. Many Germans believed that, whatever the cost, Germany must once again become an empire.

An anti-Semitic caricature published by the Nazi press with this caption: "The Jew wants the war, the peoples do not/The people bleed and the Jews are victorious."

The Nazi Beliefs

The Germany Josef Mengele grew up in placed heavy emphasis on nationalism, hatred of Jews, and the importance of German superiority. Hatred of Jews, or anti-Semitism, has occurred for thousands of years throughout the world. This hatred stems from differences in religious beliefs. Anti-Semitism is spread largely through literature. Literary works can influence any nation's interests, beliefs, and philosophies.

Several anti-Semitic works were written before and during the time of Mengele's youth, World War I, and the German depression. German anti-Semitic works were written by respected doctors, professors, politicians, and even religious leaders such as Martin Luther. Luther founded the Lutheran church and spoke against the Jews because they would not accept Jesus as their savior.

The German hatred of Jews was also politically driven. Many Germans believed that because Jews followed their own rules and customs, they were a threat to a structured German society. Because of Jewish religious practices, Jewish people seemed different from non-Jewish Germans. Germans felt especially threatened by the fact that German Jews were finding their way into prominent and powerful positions in German society.

Widespread paranoia led to rumors about Jewish plots to take over the world. Seeking to heighten this paranoia, some highly influential anti-Semitic books were published and sold in vast numbers. The books helped to establish the acceptance of strong anti-Semitism in Germany. Anti-Semitic political works were being written as early as 1905, six years before Mengele was born and more than ten years before the German depression. Thirty years later, Germany would turn into a country that practiced anti-Semitism on a large and murderous scale.

During the time of Josef Mengele's youth, there was also a strong emphasis on evolutionary philosophies, one in particular being Darwinism. Darwin's theory of evolution states that the strong survive and the weak perish. Scientists began to apply Darwinism to human beings, which is called Social Darwinism. Beginning in the late 1800s, scientists researched ways to improve the human species. This research brought about a new science called eugenics.

Eugenic scientists believed that the careful breeding of humans would lead to a stronger, more perfect human species. Scientists looked for ways of breeding stronger humans and avoiding weaker offspring. It was believed that people with physical and mental disabilities made the human species weaker. Soon, in many parts of the world including the United States, the sterilization of physically and mentally challenged people became commonplace. When a person is sterilized, he or she can no longer have children. It was thought that by sterilizing those with disabilities, all weaknesses in humans could be eliminated.

Several important Germans took the tenets of eugenics and applied them to Germany on a nationalist level. They believed that Germany should have an empire again, and that the German people were genetically superior. They wanted to separate Germans from the rest of the human species. In addition, many Germans believed that non-Germans—and Jews, in particular—were weak. Jewish people were no longer thought of as religiously different, but also as racially different.

In the late 1800s, German books and articles were published that outlined a battle of survival between Jews and Aryans. The German definition of Aryan was a person from northern Europe having blond hair and blue eyes. The idea that the German, or Aryan, race was locked in battle with other races for survival would become the main obsession of the Nazi movement in years to come.

Josef's Early Years

Being raised in the wake of World War I was difficult for most of the German population. Many middle-class households went without food and money. Josef Mengele was raised in a less burdened household because his family was upper class. His family did not suffer during the depression as others did—in fact, his family profited in the years following World War I.

Josef was born to Karl and Walburga Mengele. He was the eldest of three sons. The family lived in Günzburg, which is a small picturesque German town located on the banks of the Danube River. His parents owned a foundry that made farming equipment. When Josef was born, Karl already had more than ten people working for the company.

Josef's parents felt a strong sense of German nationalism. When World War I started in 1914, Karl left to serve in the war.

During this time, Walburga ran the foundry business. She was a fierce and talented businesswoman. She established a manufacturing contract with the German Kaiser. The contract arranged for the foundry to produce military vehicles for the war effort. The Mengeles were able to indulge their nationalist feelings and make a handsome profit as well.

Josef Mengele's parents owned a foundry that manufactured farm equipment.

One of Josef's favorite things to do was to ride the horses that were used to deliver the military vehicles to the railway. The army wagons were destined for the war front. At an early age, Josef was well aware of his family's contribution to the war effort. At the end of the war in 1918, when many businesses went under, the Mengele foundry easily returned to the peacetime production of farm machinery.

Due to the demands of running a business, Josef's parents were often absent from his life. In his memoirs, Mengele wrote that his father was a cold man, and that his mother was not very good at loving. Josef learned that relationships within his family were not based on love, but on respect. Josef grew to respect his mother's strong will and decisiveness. When his parents were around, the three brothers competed for their parents' attention. Josef developed a strong yearning for attention and fame because of the rivalry.

Many of Josef's early years were spent with his nanny Monika. She was a devout Catholic who did not allow Josef—a curious youth—to question the Catholic faith. Josef was reminded that he was named after the father of Christ, like many of his relatives had been. Despite the strictness and lack of love in Josef's life, he was known as a fun-loving child. In his memoirs, Mengele revealed that his sunny personality might have been a mask to cover deep inner suffering and unhappiness.

Teenage Josef

As a teenager, Josef was able to find some happiness by doing well in school. Although he wasn't at the top of his classes, Josef earned praise from his teachers for his self-discipline and self-control. He was a well-behaved student earning high marks for conduct and punctuality. His favorite subjects in school were biology, physics, and zoology. His favorite subject—one that became part of his life's work—was anthropology. Anthropology is the study of humans.

Josef developed into what many people thought was a striking, well-rounded teen. He was charming, confident, and comfortable with people. He had highly developed social skills for his age. He maintained a well-groomed appearance and wore tailored clothes from an early age. Josef also joined a patriotic youth group called the *Grossdeutscher Jugendbund.*

2. The Nazi Answer

By the 1920s, the Mengele foundry was one of the largest farming equipment manufacturers in Germany. The Mengele family dominated the town of Günzburg. The refined and intelligent Josef enjoyed his popularity, but also yearned to make a name for himself outside of his family's greatness. He not only wanted to succeed, he wanted fame. He once told a friend that someday the name Josef Mengele would be in the encyclopedia.

Just before 1920, the swastika, a symbol soon to be used by the Nazis, made its appearance in Munich, a city in which Mengele would soon reside. The *Thule-Gesellschaft*, a conservative political organization, decided to use the symbol in an attempt to unite people behind the idea of German nationalism. Munich soon became the center for new political groups. Many new groups blamed Jews and foreigners for the German depression. Munich was also the place where the political strength of the future Nazi Führer, Adolf Hitler, took root.

Hitler in Munich

In 1919, a conservative political party was founded in Munich called the German Workers' Party, or DAP. The goal of this party was the formation of a strong nationalist German state that would be influenced by middle-class interests. The hope was also that the German state would be entirely purged of Jews. Adolf Hitler attended a meeting of DAP and decided to join. There were around fifty members at the time.

Hitler was a fiery speaker who set DAP apart from other nationalist groups. Within a year, because of Hitler's ability to move his audiences, nearly 2,000 people were attending meetings. As early as 1920, Hitler was demanding that the citizenship of German Jews be taken away. He preached that Germany should be a vast Aryan empire void of non-Aryans and foreigners. He also called for the breaking of the Versailles Treaty. Hitler's words struck a chord in many Germans and by 1921, over 6,000 people were attending the meetings. The DAP changed its name to the Nationalsozialistische Deutsche Arbeiterpartei or the National Socialist German Workers' Party. Its members soon became known as Nazis, which is short for Nationalsozialistische.

Hitler worked hard to develop his propaganda by studying racial and political theories. When Hitler developed his philosophy of national socialism, hatred of Jews was not new, but the fact that Hitler was calling for the destruction of Jewish influence was new. Over the next few years, Hitler continued to campaign for the Nazi cause. His group established many military-like

Storm troopers and university students destroy
"un-German" books in a public burning.

divisions, including the *Sturmabteilung*, or
Storm Troopers (SA), which Josef Mengele
would join eleven years later. Members of the
SA, also known as the Brown Shirts, were
notorious for attacking Jews and anyone who
spoke against Hitler or the Nazis.

In 1923, Hitler was injured and arrested
during a Nazi attempt to overthrow the Bavarian
government. He was put on trial, which brought

national attention to him and the Nazi party. He accepted full responsibility for the failed overthrow and managed to use the attention from the trial to further Nazi propaganda.

Hitler was sentenced to five years in prison, of which he served only nine months. While he was in prison, he dictated his political manifesto, *Mein Kampf,* or *My Struggle. Mein Kampf* became one of the twentieth century's most influential works, selling millions of copies in less than ten years. The work had a huge influence on many Germans, and made desperately needed promises during this time of German economic and political weakness.

Mein Kampf emphasized Social Darwinism and racial theory. Hitler stated that some races create civilization while other races destroy it. He stated that the Jews were a destructive race, and must be removed from Germany. During the next six years, Hitler and the Nazi party spread their beliefs through rigorous campaigning and by attacking all political opposition.

Mengele in Munich

Josef passed his school exams in 1930. Being the eldest son, he was first in line to work at the family business. But Josef was driven by his desire to make a name for himself, so he looked into other careers. At one point, he considered becoming a dentist, since his town lacked one. He reasoned that he would be highly valued and respected.

Ultimately, Josef decided on medicine. Josef had been influenced by Germany's interest in eugenics and racial theory, and decided to focus his studies on anthropology and human genetics. He told a friend that by focusing on these fields, he could study the entire range of medicine. A wave of interest in genetics was sweeping through the intellectual world, and Josef hoped to make his mark. He also hoped that by becoming the first scientist in his family, he would earn the respect of his parents.

Josef left his family and moved to Munich in October of 1930 in order to attend Munich

University. Munich was brimming with Nazi activity at the time. The movement had spread throughout the rest of Germany as well. The Nazis had become the second largest political party in the German parliament. Josef was fully exposed to the Nazi movement. He took a keen interest in the philosophies of Alfred Rosenberg, a philosopher of the Nazi movement. In 1930, Rosenberg published his book *The Myth of the Twentieth Century*, which sold millions of copies. His book promoted the racist idea that Germans must keep German blood pure from racial contamination. Sixteen years later, Rosenberg would be hanged for crimes against humanity.

At the university, Josef showed more of an interest in learning about evolution and cultural origins than in treating the ill. In addition to his studies, Josef was attracted to political issues. He joined the youth wing of the *Stahlhelm*, or Steel Helmets, in 1931 at the age of twenty. The Steel Helmets was a nationalistic, anti-Semitic group founded in 1918 by World War I veterans. Josef

Alfred Rosenberg, who elevated the theory of
Nordic supremacy to the level of a religion,
addresses a crowd in 1920.

liked the group's military style and strong sense
of nationalism. On October 11, 1931, an alliance
was formed between the Nazis, the Steel
Helmets, and other nationalist groups, with the
goal of making Germany a dominant empire,
free of what they considered racial burdens.

During the same year that Josef joined the
Steel Helmets, Josef's father, Karl, decided to
join the Nazi party. He saw a bright future for

the Nazi movement. One of Karl's companions was the chief of the local Nazi party, which had already driven out the 300 or so Jews who lived in Günzburg. Karl's Nazi involvement brought Hitler to Günzburg a year later for a speech at the Mengele factory. In the years to follow, Karl was made a town council member and his business boomed, employing more than 350 people, all thanks to his Nazi connections.

Baldur von Schirach, leader of the Hitler Youth, salutes his troops at a review parade in Nuremberg.

Hitler Comes Into Power

By 1933, Adolf Hitler was named chancellor of Germany. The German parliament hoped that by giving him this position, Hitler could be controlled and a Nazi overthrow of the parliament could be avoided. In this position, however, Hitler was able to change the system from within. By the end of 1933, many laws were passed that would help the Nazis to establish the Third Reich.

The Third Reich, which means the third kingdom, was the name for Germany under Nazi control. The Nazis saw the Holy Roman Empire as the First Reich, and the German Empire from 1871–1918 as the Second Reich. Hitler wanted the Third Reich to dominate Europe. He envisioned that the so-called lesser races would be used as slave laborers for the master Aryan race.

Many scientists and academics helped Hitler to develop his national socialist philosophies into laws. One of these scientists, Dr. Ernst

Rudin, was a strong influence on Josef. Josef regularly attended Dr. Rudin's lectures while at school. Rudin helped draw up the sterilization laws that Hitler enacted in July 1933.

Rudin held the radical belief that doctors should destroy any life that had no value. Rudin believed that people had no value if they suffered from alcoholism, blindness, deafness, epilepsy, mental disorders, physical malformations, mental slowness, or disease. He hoped that by killing people with these characteristics, the quality of the German race would improve. This was also known as "racial hygiene." Mengele was exposed to many respected professionals whose beliefs on race reflected Dr. Rudin's views.

◆　◆　◆

Hitler established the first concentration camp, Dachau, within the first few months of 1933. The purpose of the concentration camp was to imprison anyone who opposed the Third Reich. It was also a place where Hitler could send the undesirables or "asocials" of German society. Asocials were deemed to be people who were a burden or harmful to German society.

The first inmates of the camp were Communists, Democrats, and powerful Jews such as officials, journalists, and lawyers. The "asocials" who were sent there included criminals, homosexuals, alcoholics, Jehovah's witnesses, beggars, vagrants, and mentally and physically challenged people. The concentration camp was meant to ensure that the Nazis would not be opposed in their drive to control all of Germany.

Hitler also quickly established harsh racial policies. The Nazis developed a nation-wide system of defining Jewish ancestry on the basis of a German's bloodline. People with both German and Jewish ancestors were called *Mischlinge*, or half-breeds. There were immediate boycotts on all Jewish and *Mischlinge* shops and businesses. Jews were forced to quit all civil service jobs and

A member of the SA stands in front of a Jewish-owned
department store where a boycott sign reads: "Germans
defend yourselves; don't buy from Jews!"

important positions. Jews were turned away from school and denied basic liberties. Hitler started Aryanization, which was the taking over of Jewish businesses and jobs by non-Jewish Germans.

As Mengele was studying medicine, German Nazi leaders were looking to those with medical expertise to make the new Germany a reality. By 1934, Hitler established the racial hygiene policy throughout Germany. A sterilization law was created, called the Law for the Prevention of Genetically Diseased Offspring, which made all doctors responsible for reporting and sterilizing all Germans with genetic defects.

The German president died in 1934 and Hitler assumed total power over Germany. Soon it was accepted that some lives were not worth living, or that some people were unworthy of life. Along with the sterilization law, a euthanasia program was developed in order to free Germany from taking care of the unworthy. People deemed worthless were killed in the euthanasia program. This was cruelly believed to relieve these people of their suffering. Hitler's emphasis on a medical solution to Germany's problems brought those in the medical profession to the forefront. Many of Josef Mengele's teachers were swept up in the powerful force of the Nazi movement; soon Mengele would be as well.

Members of the SA celebrate Hitler's assumption of power as chancellor at a torchlight parade.

Mengele Becomes a Doctor and a Nazi

Mengele worked ambitiously for a doctorate in anthropology while also pursuing a degree in medicine. Between 1934 and 1938, Mengele wrote papers on heredity and genetics in relation to racial groups. Although his thinking was right in line with the Nazi ideas of race and genetics, his works were surprisingly void of anti-Semitic themes. The papers were more scientific than racist.

In 1936, Mengele passed his final examinations in Munich. He landed his first paid job in the university medical clinic at Leipzig. Mengele worked long hours as a beginning doctor but still found the time to fall in love. He met a professor's daughter named Irene Schoenbein, his future first wife and mother of his son, Rolf. Life as a doctor did not please Mengele. He yearned to return to his research studies in genetics. On the recommendation of a Leipzig professor,

Mengele was transferred to the Third Reich's Institute of Hereditary Biology and Race Research.

At the institute, he was given a research assistant position under one of Europe's most important genetic scientists, Otmar Freiherr von Verschuer. Dr. von Verschuer founded the institute in 1934. Dr. von Verschuer was an admirer of Hitler and the role of medicine in the Third Reich. Von Verschuer believed that the science of eugenics would come to full bloom under Nazi leadership. The young, twenty-six-year-old Mengele developed a strong respect for Dr. von Verschuer's beliefs, which undoubtedly influenced Mengele to follow his urge to join the Nazi party.

After a four-year ban on joining the Nazi Party, Mengele was allowed to apply in 1937. Hitler had restricted membership in the party in 1933 because he feared that too many liberals would want to join. He believed that these people would weaken the party's strength. After being accepted by the Nazi

Party, Mengele applied for membership in the most elite group of the party, the SS, or *Schutzstaffel,* which means protection squad. The SS controlled all German police agencies and was responsible for guarding Germany's racial purity. Mengele's family history was inspected, and after it became clear to the Nazis that he was a "pure" German, he was allowed to join.

Although all SS members were ordered to get a tattoo signifying their membership and blood type, Josef managed to avoid the tattoo. He did not want his perfect skin to be marred. He also joined the *Nationalsozialistischer Deutscher Ärztebund,* which was the Nazi physicians' association. Membership in the Nazi Party complemented his research work at the institute, which was to study the importance of heredity in relation to the Nazi goal of racial hygiene.

3. Becoming a Nazi Doctor

In the years following his appointment to the institute, Mengele followed Nazi beliefs. By the end of 1938, he was a full-fledged member of the Nazi Party and a licensed doctor of medicine. To assure his success as an SS officer, Mengele left his research in 1938 to attend three months of training with the German army. When training ended, he was sent to his first posting in the Snalfedon-Tirol mountain region, where he served until the end of his posting. Then he returned to his research work.

In 1939, Mengele married Irene after a Nazi search into her ancestral background had been conducted. The race of her grandfather was not known, and it was proposed that he might be Jewish. Irene's Aryan appearance, with blond hair and Nordic features, finally swayed officials to allow the marriage. Mengele was disappointed that he could not prove Irene's Aryan ancestry. This meant that their names wouldn't be added to a Nazi book called *Sippenbuch,* or kinship book. Acceptance into the book meant that a family was racially pure and Aryan.

While finishing his studies in Frankfurt, Mengele also wrote reviews of academic books about heredity. He asserted that many of the books did not place enough emphasis on the superiority of the German race. Mengele was now completely under the power of the Nazi movement. He believed that Hitler was the one man who could save the human race from self-destruction. A few weeks after Mengele's wedding in 1939, Hitler started a war in the belief that he could do just that.

Early War, Young Doctor

During the years that Mengele spent at the institute, Hitler was able to bring all aspects of German life under Nazi domination. The German police and all government offices were under Nazi control. He established Nazi schools for the German youth, so Nazi education could start early. Hitler also worked to dehumanize Jews and asocials; if his followers saw Jews and "asocials" as less than human, it would be easier to get rid of them. The sterilization and euthanasia programs were expanded so that tens of thousands of patients could be treated for racial hygiene.

On November 9, 1938, an attack on the remaining Jewish populations in Germany, Austria, and parts of Czechoslovakia occurred. Jewish people were assaulted and murdered and Jewish businesses and synagogues were burned. This attack is called *Kristallnacht*, or the "Night of Broken Glass." It marked the murderous beginning of Hitler's solution to Germany's problems. Over thirty thousand male Jews were sent to concentration camps during *Kristallnacht*.

Aside from ridding the German Empire of Jews and the so-called asocials, another goal of Hitler's was that Germany would acquire land from neighboring territories. He felt that the German people needed and deserved more *Lebensraum,* or living space. Conquered territories would provide extra space for living and farming. Having more territory would also help the Third Reich assure its dominance over Europe. Of course, this land wouldn't be handed over freely; it would have to be taken by force.

Germany had already annexed Austria and Czechoslovakia, and on September 1, 1939, Hitler and the German army invaded Poland. This was the start of World War II. Two days later, Great Britain and France declared war on Germany because of its move against Poland. When Germany took over Poland, it also in-herited the two million Jews who lived there. As more territories were conquered, more Jews and "asocials" would have to be dealt with. Within a month of the invasion, plans to establish ghettos throughout Poland were underway.

Ghettos were heavily guarded, enclosed sub-cities that were designed to hold people that Hitler wanted removed from the German Empire. All Jews of conquered territories would be sent to the ghettos, and then on to concentration camps. Ghettos were overcrowded and unsanitary. Jews in the ghettos were forced to wear armbands that marked their Jewish identity. Anyone caught without an armband was executed immediately.

In October 1939, Hitler established an area in Poland to serve as an administrative center of government for the conquered territory. In the not-too-distant future, the Nazis would build many of their death camps in this area. Death camps were a key part of the Nazi plan to destroy Jews and "asocials." These camps were used for large-scale murder.

◆ ◆ ◆

At the outbreak of the war, Mengele was suffering from a kidney ailment. His health

Young Jewish women sell armbands on
the streets of the Warsaw ghetto.

condition forced him to wait until July of 1940 before joining the war service. He saw the war as Germany's chance to create a dominant Aryan empire. His first post was as a medical officer in an army unit. A month later, Mengele transferred to a special wing of the SS called the *Waffen* SS, which was the largest branch of the SS. *Waffen* SS members were soldiers who fought at the war front, seeing much bloodshed.

Heinrich Himmler (left) inspects the concentration camp in Mauthausen, Austria, on April 27, 1941.

During the first few months of 1941, Mengele was stationed in occupied Poland, where he worked at the Race and Resettlement Office. He worked under the direct orders of Heinrich Himmler. Himmler was the leader of the entire SS. He was a very powerful man in the Nazi movement who also oversaw the camps. Himmler believed that Germany would be rid of the Jewish problem once Germany exterminated all Jews. He felt that killing Jews was a German right.

Becoming a Soldier

Prior to the German occupation of Poland, the Nazis established a division of the SS called the SS *Einsatzgruppen*, or action squads. The *Einsatzgruppen* were well-armed, mobile murdering squads. They were used during the invasion of Poland to kill hundreds of Polish Jews and Catholic intellectuals. The units were assigned to kill anyone who was not racially "pure" or who posed a threat to the Nazi Empire.

FOUR POINT PLAN

Himmler created a four-point program that Mengele and other SS doctors were to follow while conducting studies. Mengele was to examine the racial strength of the Polish people who were to occupy the newly conquered territories. The Nazis would allow only pro-Nazi, non-Jewish Polish people of German descent to live in these territories. Mengele followed Himmler's four-point program, and he, along with other Nazi doctors, was responsible for making sure that it was carried out:

- Territories were to be cleansed of non-Germans by whatever means available.

- Persons claiming German ancestry were to be examined and classified according to racial characteristics. Those with questionable ancestry would be separated and were to live under special conditions to ensure good behavior toward the German Empire.

- People who looked like Germans were to undergo racial examinations to see if their ancestors were originally from Germany, but had resettled. People discovered to have German ancestry would be sent to Germany for German reeducation.

- Orphans and children in public care were also to be evaluated.

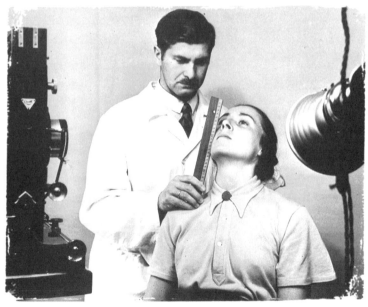

A doctor measures the facial features of a young German woman during a racial examination.

In June of 1941, Germany invaded the Soviet Union. Three thousand *Einsatzgruppen* soldiers went into the Soviet Union to kill Jews and Russian officials rather than transport them to ghettos or camps. The *Einsatzgruppen* soldiers were known for their ruthless massacres, which many people witnessed with horror. Many of these killings were brutal and sadistic, such as smashing children's skulls against walls while

55

swinging them by their ankles. The *Einsatzgruppen* were responsible for more than one million Jewish deaths during the Holocaust. Many members of other German troop divisions, including the *Waffen* SS, were invited and encouraged to witness the brutal killings carried out by the *Einsatzgruppen.*

◆ ◆ ◆

At the time of the invasion of the Soviet Union, Mengele was posted to service in the Ukraine, which was part of the Soviet Union. Within just a few days of his posting there, Mengele was awarded a medal called the Iron Cross for his actions during dangerous battlefield conditions. Mengele was transferred to the medical corps of the *Waffen* SS Viking division in January of 1942. This division went further into Russian territory than any other German army unit.

By July, Mengele's division had moved up to the front line for a bloody battle against the

Russian army that lasted five days. Mengele was awarded another medal for his soldiering during this battle. He was awarded a first class Iron Cross for rescuing two German soldiers from a burning tank. While fighting on the Russian front, Mengele was injured. Due to his injury, Mengele was declared unfit for further action.

As 1942 came to a close, Mengele was transferred to Berlin to work at the Race and Resettlement Office. By this time, he had been decorated with four war medals—two Iron Crosses, the Black Badge for the Wounded, and the Medal for the Care of the German People. He was the only Nazi doctor to have earned such a collection of medals and was promoted to the rank of *Hauptsturmführer*, or captain.

The Final Solution to the Jewish Question

While Mengele was serving in the *Waffen* SS, plans for the Final Solution were being carried out in the German Third Reich. The Final Solution was a horrific plan that the Nazis believed would rid Germany of Jews forever. The plan outlined the systematic murder of every single European Jew. It was often referred to as "the Final Solution to the Jewish question."

Although historians aren't sure of the exact date on which the Final Solution started, recently discovered documents offer proof that it began in June of 1941. The first public mention of the Final Solution occurred ten years earlier in a newspaper article in the *Munich Post*, but it suggested a different means to that end. The Final Solution of 1931 was a plan to remove Jews from German society through slave labor.

Heinrich Himmler—under whom Mengele served in Poland—played a key role in the creation of the Final Solution plan of 1941. A year earlier, in May of 1940, he drew up a memorandum that called for the removal of Jews by any means necessary. It stated that extermination of Jews was not impossible. By using the term "extermination" rather than the word "murder," Himmler furthered the idea that Jews were subhuman and that it was acceptable to kill them. The memorandum was given to Hitler, who read the paper and authorized it to become a directive. Hitler asked Himmler to notify key Nazi leaders of the new directive.

The idea of the Final Solution was passed to Hermann Göring, who was a key figure of the Third Reich. Göring then authorized Reinhard Heydrich, another Nazi leader, to carry out the Final Solution to the Jewish question. The Final Solution was to be used in all parts of German-dominated Europe.

No written details were ever found that stated how Hitler wished the Final Solution to be carried out. Historians assume that Hitler's right-hand men did their best to interpret how he wanted it done. This included the increased action of the killing squads, more efforts to establish death camps, and the deportation of Jews to death camps for immediate extermination. By the end of the year, several death camps were in full operation and had already carried out the murder of several thousand Jews, Gypsies, and prisoners of war, and "asocials."

4. Doctors, Madmen, and the Angel of Death

The killings done by the SS troops, particularly the *Einsatzgruppen,* or killing squads, were gruesome to witness. Some victims, including children, were not killed instantly when they were shot and clung to life, screaming and covered in blood. Many *Einsatzgruppen* soldiers had difficulty coping with their task. Several members committed suicide rather than live with the knowledge of what they had done. It soon became obvious to Nazi leaders that the responsibility of carrying out the Final Solution was too much for these young men to bear. Nazi leaders looked for less gruesome ways to murder the Nazi enemies. They turned their efforts toward the death camps, and looked for more methodical ways to kill.

◆　◆　◆

In the summer of 1942, Mengele's friend and mentor Dr. von Verschuer was named director of the Kaiser Wilhelm Institute for Anthropology, Human Genetics, and Eugenics in Berlin. This was a few months before Mengele's transfer to Berlin. As director of the institute, von Verschuer oversaw research programs for German racial purity. Many of the research projects involved the use of twins in order to have a way of comparing test results. Mengele soon contacted von Verschuer and said that he would work at the institute during his free time while posted in Berlin.

The Final Solution was well underway by the time Mengele reached Berlin. The Nazis did not publicize their plans for the Final Solution. The purpose of the secrecy was to get full cooperation from everyone, especially the victims. The Nazi doctors, however, did know of the concentration and death camps, and several Nazi doctors were already experimenting on camp prisoners. Soon the Nazi doctors would become a crucial part of the Final Solution.

The Organization of Death

It's likely that von Verschuer encouraged the thirty-two-year-old Mengele to apply for a post at Auschwitz, the largest concentration death camp. Mengele would have an unlimited supply of test subjects there, and the freedom to carry out any kind of research project. Furthermore, Mengele would have access to a group of people that was very important to his and von Verschuer's research—twins.

Mengele arrived at Auschwitz on May 30, 1943. Soon after Mengele's arrival, von Verschuer applied for and received grants for the studies that he and Mengele would continue carrying out. Mengele would send specimens from Auschwitz to von Verschuer in Berlin, and their research work would continue.

The Auschwitz camp was a nightmarish world unto itself. The construction of the Auschwitz concentration camp began in 1940. Over the next five years, a forced labor camp and a death camp were built. The

Railroad tracks leading to Auschwitz

camp was located in the town where the former Polish military had trained, so it was already well suited to house many people. The camp was also located near the major railroad lines of Poland, so trains loaded with prisoners would have easy access.

The camp spread out over a few miles and had three main sections. Auschwitz I was the concentration and main camp. Auschwitz II, also called Auschwitz-Birkenau, was the death camp. Auschwitz III, also called Monowitz-Buna, was a forced-labor camp. There were also several sub-camps located within a few miles of the enormous Auschwitz camp.

Duties of a Death Camp Doctor

Nazi leaders decided that death by gassing was the least gruesome and most efficient way to exterminate prisoners. Death camps were

City of Death

A Hungarian Jewish prisoner of Auschwitz named Dr. Miklos Nyiszli had the misfortune of knowing and working with Josef Mengele. Nyiszli was allowed to live because he was a doctor, and doctors were needed to help with the Nazis' medical experiments. When Dr. Mengele first arrived at the camp, he asked Dr. Nyiszli to accompany him on a tour through Auschwitz. Up until this point, Dr. Nyiszli had only seen the small section of the camp in which he was forced to live. When Mengele showed him the rest of the camp, Nyiszli was amazed and terrified by the size of Auschwitz. At the time of Mengele's arrival, Auschwitz held more than 130,000 prisoners, and exterminated over 5,000 people a day.

established to carry out the gassings with great efficiency. From the *Selektionens* to the disposing of the bodies, the Nazi doctors were involved at every stage of the gassings.

Most Nazi doctors at Auschwitz, except for doctors who had specific duties such as taking care of SS members, were required to take part in the gassings. Nazi leaders and doctors designed the stages of the gassings to be misleading to the prisoners. Every action that the Nazi soldiers and doctors performed was part of a cruel hoax that lead the prisoners quickly and quietly to their deaths.

Upon exiting the train at Auschwitz, the prisoners formed the line for the *Selektionen.* When a prisoner was chosen by a Nazi doctor to go to the left, the prisoner was told that he or she would be taking a shower in the bathhouse. Many of the doctors on duty at the *Selektionen* made a show of acting polite and pretended to be concerned for the well-being of the prisoners.

Prisoners were instructed to follow the line to the bathhouse. Those too weak to walk were put into vehicles. After the *Selektionen* was finished, the *Selektionen* doctor was driven to the building where the gassings took place. The doctor was driven in a vehicle painted with a Red Cross to make it appear that this was a humane procedure carried out by medical professionals. Another part of the hoax was that other prisoners from the labor camp were selected to help in the process. It seemed impossible that prisoners would lead other prisoners to their deaths, but in order to avoid their own death, they did so by the thousands.

Once the prisoners were lured into the building marked "bathhouse," the building was locked from the outside. The doctor

Nazi soldiers divide a transport of Hungarian Jews into groups to be sent either to the labor camp (right) or to the gas chamber (left). The line to the gas chamber is the longer of the two.

determined how many pellets of gas would be needed to kill the prisoners. The doctor also selected one officer out of a special group called disinfectors. A disinfector was a medical technician whose duty was to drop the poisonous pellets inside the locked chamber. The doctor would sometimes observe how the prisoners were dying.

After the prisoners were dead, the doctor gave the order to open and air out the chamber. He then noted the amount of time that it had taken for the prisoners to die and signed a form verifying their deaths. Lastly, the doctor made sure that the bodies were burned in the crematorium. The crematorium was connected to the gas chamber. Burning the bodies was done in part to erase the evidence that millions of murders were taking place.

On a clear day, the billowing smoke of burning bodies from the crematoriums could be seen thirty miles from Auschwitz. The burning flesh produced a constant stench, which Mengele's wife asked about when she visited the camp. Mengele told Irene not to ask about such matters, which abruptly ended the discussion about the sickening smell of Auschwitz.

The gassings occurred several times a day during the twenty months that Mengele served at Auschwitz. During this time, Mengele not only presided over his own

Canisters of the gas Zyklon B that the Nazis used for mass murder

Selektionen, but would show up when he wasn't scheduled for *Selektionen.* Survivors of Auschwitz remember that Mengele was one of the few doctors who didn't need liquor or drugs to help him get through the selection process. Many doctors reported to duty drunk or high in an attempt to cope with the *Selektionen* tasks. Mengele showed up for *Selektionen* duty with enthusiasm, even though the process sent hundreds of thousands of people to their deaths.

Doctor Mengele Excels

In a place where the doctors were expected to cause death, there was little that Mengele could do to fail. In fact, Mengele excelled in the environment at Auschwitz. He took on any extra challenges that he could. He proved that he fully agreed with the Nazi movement and its Final Solution. He also proved that he had no problems using the gas chambers to solve any situations that came up.

Within a month of Mengele's arrival, the Gypsy prisoner camp had an outbreak of typhus, which is a disease that spreads quickly. Mengele's solution was to send more than one thousand Gypsies to the gas chambers. He spared only Gypsies of German ancestry. Gypsies were European people who traveled and didn't own land or have steady jobs. Nazis didn't hate Gypsies as much as Jews but still saw them as a threat to an ordered way of life. There are conflicting reports about how Mengele felt about Gypsies. Some people believe that he was kind to them, while others—who cite this mass killing as an example—say that Mengele hated the Gypsies as much as he hated the Jews.

A few months later, the women's camp had an outbreak of typhus as well. Mengele sent all of the Jewish inhabitants of one barrack—more than 600 women—to the gas chamber. He did this to cleanse the barracks of typhus. He then moved other infected women in to treat them in the clean barracks. He had each emptied barracks completely "cleansed" in order to rid the camp of typhus. During this time, he became infected with typhus himself, but soon recovered. Auschwitz doctor Eduard Wirths felt that Mengele deserved the War Service Medal for finding a solution to the typhus epidemic.

A Symbol of Auschwitz

Many survivors remember Mengele as a horrible figure who came to symbolize Auschwitz. Others remember that in contrast to the weak, dirty prisoners, Mengele, with his immaculate, almost perfect looks, stood out like a movie star. In survivors' and colleagues' memories, Mengele ranges from being a gentleman to a murderous madman. Many people believe that Mengele was both. His breeding had given him what appeared to be a refined nature, while his reverence for the Nazis allowed him to heartlessly follow grisly orders.

Sixteen months into his posting at Auschwitz, the chief physician evaluated

Mengele's work. Mengele was commended for his outstanding service. The evaluation went on to say that even though Mengele was a strict soldier, he was also popular and respected by his SS peers. There is little doubt that Mengele enjoyed his duties. He conducted the *Selektionen* with precision and speed. He uttered "right" or "left" within a few seconds of seeing each prisoner. One prisoner called him "the Lord of life or death." Soon he was known simply as the Angel of Death. His military record separated him from other Nazi doctors who had no war experience. He wore his war medals proudly and maintained military bearing and behavior.

Auschwitz leaders made life in the camps as comfortable as possible for Nazi officers like Mengele. There were orchestras made up of prisoner musicians, that played during the *Selektionen* and throughout the camp. The orchestras were used both to make the prisoners believe that it was a peaceful camp and to entertain the Nazi officers. The camp

Prisoners who were musicians were selected for prison orchestras to entertain Nazi officers.

also had a swimming pool, theater, library, soccer stadium, and bar—all for SS members only. A few Nazi leaders had their families living within the camp in nice homes. Some Nazi families even tended gardens and kept pets.

Although some survivors remember Mengele as being almost everywhere at once, Mengele had his own laboratory block and his

75

own medical staff. The staff was mostly made up of prisoners who had medical expertise, such as technicians, nurses, and doctors. He was not overly kind to his staff—many of them were Jews. Occasionally, however, he lost sight of that fact and treated some of them as colleagues. They had lively discussions about the nature of the research and the findings from the studies. But one wrong word in the conversation and Mengele would return to treating staff members like subhumans.

Even with his duties of *Selektionen* and his own research, Mengele found time to take part in the labor camp activities. After the *Selektionen,* about two out of every fifteen people were sent to the labor camp. The rest (thirteen out of every fifteen) were sent to the gas chambers. Those who made it to the labor camp were literally worked to death. Many strong-spirited prisoners worked well past exhaustion. Labor camp *Selektionen* were established in order to weed out these workers as their energy drained away.

During labor *Selektionen,* prisoners were forced to stand in organized lines for hours, sometimes in the freezing cold. At some *Selektionen,* the prisoners were asked to undress completely so that the doctors could easily examine the prisoner's physical condition. Within a few seconds, the doctors decided which prisoners were to be sent to the gas chambers. It was a morbid replaying of the moment when the prisoners had first arrived at Auschwitz. Mengele was present at many of the labor camp *Selektionen.*

5. Crimes Without Punishment—The Nazi Doctor

There were over seventy different medical research experiments done in the camps. More than two hundred Nazi doctors conducted two main categories of experiments—one for military purposes and one for the purposes of racial hygiene. Military experiments were done to aid Germany's war effort. Racial experiments were done to prove that other races were inferior, to keep other races from breeding, and to advance the Aryan race.

In both categories of experiments, prisoners became subjects against their will. Most of the experiments were brutal and done without painkillers. Some experiments were done merely to satisfy morbid medical curiosity, such

Military Experiments

The Nazis made a great deal of effort to gain the advantage on the battlefield. The medical experiments on prisoners were done in the hopes of helping German soldiers to survive on the front lines. The experiments were brutal, and usually led to the deaths of the prisoners.

AMPUTATIONS—Limbs of prisoners were cut off to see how fast blood flowed from live, alert humans. This was done in hopes of finding ways of slowing blood flow from wounds.

FREEZING EXPERIMENTS—Prisoners were immersed in freezing water to see how long they could survive before dying.

TRANSPLANTS—The limbs were cut off of two prisoners and switched to see if transplants could work.

WOUND EXPERIMENTS—Prisoners were given wounds as well as bacterial infections to simulate wounds received at the battlefront. Patients were then treated with experimental medications in attempts to cure the infections.

as answering the question, "What if a baby was deprived of its mother's milk . . . how long might it live?" Autopsies—examinations of deceased prisoners—were also a part of the experiments. This meant that the death of the patient was an expected stage of the experiment.

Mengele's Experiments

Dr. Mengele's experiments were conducted for purposes of racial hygiene and were as gruesome as the military experiments. Most of the survivors from Mengele's experiments are twins. He conducted research on twins of all ages because he hoped to unlock the secrets of multiple births. With this knowledge, it was hoped that Aryans could be born in multiple numbers, and the population could quickly increase as a result. Other experiments were carried out to understand genetics. More than forty sets of prisoner twins survived Mengele's experiments and the Holocaust.

The Nazis used Jews and prisoners of war as guinea pigs in their first medical experiments in the Dachau concentration camp. This prisoner died during an experiment after his lungs burst.

Mengele's Twins

Mengele attended other doctors' *Selektionen* to make sure that twins were being spared from the gassings. Prisoners remember Mengele and other SS soldiers directing twins to step out of the *Selektionen,* shouting, "Twins, twins, out!" The twins were separated from the prisoners and placed in special barracks. Because they were part of the Nazi race studies, twins lived in better conditions than the labor camp prisoners. Mengele made sure that the twins were fed and taken care of.

The twins were carefully measured, X-rayed, and examined. The measurements of one twin were compared to the other's. Each twin had a file filled with research data. Because Mengele's files were never found, it is not certain what the goals of his experiments were.

The last stage of the experiment was usually an autopsy. The twins were either gassed or injected with a poison called phenol.

These twin sisters show before-and-after photos at a world gathering of survivors of Mengele's Auschwitz experiments.

Mengele and his assistants administered the deadly shots. Phenol injections had been used earlier in the war to kill prisoners. After months of experimentation with the injections, the Nazis discovered that the quickest and easiest way of administering the shot was by stabbing a syringe directly into

Mengele's Twin Experiments

Medical experiments on twins included but were not limited to:

- Sampling—Great amounts of blood or tissue were taken from some sets of twins, which caused their deaths.

- Blood transfusions—The blood of one set of twins was switched with the blood of another set of twins.

- Organ switching—The organs of one twin were switched with those of the other twin, or one set's organs were switched with the organs of another set of twins.

- Deliberate infection and poisoning—Twins were injected with diseases or poisons and their reactions were compared.

the heart. This method produced death within fifteen seconds.

Aryan Blue

Another of Mengele's bizarre experiments was focused on eye color. The ultimate Aryan was believed to have blond hair and blue eyes.

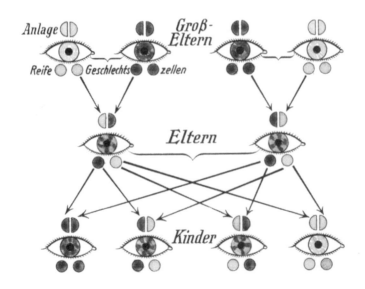

This chart, illustrating the transmission of the genetic traits for blue and brown eye-coloring over three generations, was used in a 1934 lecture series on race in Munich.

Mengele started working on seven-year-old prisoners who had blond hair and brown eyes. He injected the prisoners' eyes with chemicals and dyes such as methylene blue to see if he could change the natural coloring of the eye's iris. Mengele also did the experiment on twins and other prisoners. Some patients recovered from the injections, but others suffered infections, blindness, and, in one case, death.

Mengele's Other Experiments

Mengele experimented on prisoners who had physical abnormalities or who were abnormally short. Mengele ordered soldiers to shoot the prisoners with physical abnormalities, and their bodies were examined. At one point, Mengele found an entire family of short people at the *Selektionen*. He was very kind to them during the experiments, but when the experiments came to an end, they were gassed. Mengele's research findings, along with the bones of the dead, were sent to von Verschuer for continued study.

Mengele also sent sets of eyes to von Verschuer that were taken from the bodies of the twins, Gypsies, and other "patients." Some prisoners were deliberately killed just to harvest the eye samples, especially any Gypsy prisoners with two different colored eyes. The samples of experiments and research material were always carefully packed and shipped off by Mengele's assistants. Survivors remember menacing collections of human eyes on tables and tacked to the walls of Mengele's laboratories.

Dr. Mengele also studied a rare disease called noma. The disease caused body tissues to die around the mouth and face. The children of the Gypsy camp commonly suffered from the disease. At one point, Mengele had two of the Gypsy children killed so that he could examine their detached heads.

The End of Mengele's Experiments

Our understanding of Mengele's nature comes from surviving prisoners who served on his medical team. They remembered his ability to show civility, and yet within seconds to do something murderous. Mengele purposefully scheduled gassings of Jewish prisoners on Jewish religious holidays. He sometimes wore a pistol, which was a strange thing for a doctor to wear.

Mengele's entire goal at Auschwitz was to uphold Nazi supremacy. Some people who knew Mengele personally believed that he did horrible things only because of the Nazi movement and his faithful belief in it. One friend even believed that if the war and Nazism had never happened, Mengele might have been a harmless but slightly cruel professor at a German university—a world away from the medical monster that he became at Auschwitz.

Toward the end of 1944, the German war effort was failing. Massive Allied invasions were underway. Some German officials plotted to assassinate Hitler, but their attempt failed. The Russian army was succeeding against Germany and had managed to liberate a German death camp. The Allies had liberated several cities that had been occupied by German armies. Prisoner and ghetto revolts had taken place, even at Auschwitz. The Auschwitz prison revolt resulted in the destruction of one of the crematoriums.

Mengele's experiments were also coming to an end. Prisoner trains to Auschwitz had already begun to slow by the middle of 1944. By the end of 1944, the death camp was being dismantled and plans to evacuate the camp were underway. However, the gassings and experiments continued until the last possible moment. The final roll call at the camp was performed on January 17, 1945. A massive evacuation began the next day, when thousands of prisoners were forced to march on foot toward Austria. Other prisoners were shot, or crammed into train cars without a specific destination scheduled. Ten days after the final roll call, the Soviet armies liberated Auschwitz, freeing the last of the prisoners, who numbered nearly seven thousand.

Mengele left the camp on the same day as the final roll call. Days before leaving camp, Mengele collected all of his medical papers. He did not want them to fall into the hands of the enemy. He was assigned to another concentration camp, which he fled on

February 18 to avoid the advancing Soviet troops. While fleeing, he joined a group of retreating German forces. Mengele switched his SS uniform for one of theirs and tried to blend in among the soldiers. He met an old colleague who helped him stay with the group. Mengele gave his medical papers to a nurse he met while with the group. He believed that she would be able to hide the papers and, eventually, return them to him.

On April 30, 1945, Adolf Hitler committed suicide. Germany surrendered on May 8, 1945. On June 15, American forces captured more than ten thousand German soldiers in the same region where Mengele's group was. Mengele's group was captured a few days later. At this time, Mengele's name was listed as a principal war criminal and he was wanted for mass murder. During questioning, Mengele used his real name, but he was not identified as an SS member. He did not have the tattoo that all SS members were branded with. It's believed that the

American POW camp officials hadn't received the wanted list and therefore didn't identify him as the SS doctor.

Mengele Runs from His Past

While being detained in the American POW camp, Mengele suffered from extreme depression. He was examined by a doctor who was also a prisoner. Mengele told the doctor how he feared being discovered. The doctor, Fritz Ulmann, had access to the office that released identification papers. Dr. Ulmann made a set of identification papers in his own name for Mengele to use so that he wouldn't get caught. Although there are conflicting reports as to when Mengele was set free, it definitely happened toward the end of 1945.

He was released in a Bavarian town which was close to a town where a friend named Dr. Miller lived. He decided to walk to the nearby town. On the way, he was offered the use of a bike by a farmer who had an extra one. Along the way, Mengele hid his real identification papers in the handle of the bike. When he parted company with the farmer, he forgot about the papers. From that moment, he only had one set of papers, identifying him as Fritz Ulmann.

Because of his family's power, and the unwillingness of many Germans to believe what was being said about Nazi atrocities, many people helped Mengele evade capture. He relied on his friend Dr. Miller to relay messages to his family. He eventually fled from the Millers when he thought capture was near. He relied on another set of friends for his next lodging. They also helped him to find a safe place that was not associated with anyone he knew. He was sent to work on a farm, where he stayed until 1948. Ironically, one of his farm jobs was to select and separate good potatoes from bad potatoes.

While Mengele was in hiding, his friends and family hid the truth. His wife and family told authorities that Mengele was dead. Irene even visited Mengele while he was at the farm. Dr. von Verschuer destroyed all evidence of his correspondence with Mengele. Mengele even managed to get his medical papers back from the nurse he met while fleeing.

A New Life

In the spring of 1949, Mengele decided to leave the country in order to make a new life for himself. His wife refused to leave with him. Mengele was forced to flee alone. Mengele made his way to Argentina by using his father's vast business connections. He arrived on August 26, 1949. Mengele kept in touch and visited with his family over the years, but his marriage to Irene was finished. To his son, Rolf, he became known as Uncle Fritz. His true identity was revealed to Rolf years later.

Disappearing into Argentina was not difficult for Mengele. He found Buenos Aires to be a wonderful place, as did many other Nazi members on the run. He even joined a group of prominent Argentine leaders and resettled Nazis. Mengele worked as a salesman, selling products from his father's foundry. He even married again. His father arranged for him to marry Martha, the widow of Mengele's brother, Karl Junior. Karl Senior arranged a meeting in the Swiss Alps for Mengele, Martha, her son, and Rolf. The meeting went well, and Martha and her son eventually moved to Argentina. Martha and Mengele were married in 1958, and Mengele used his real name to apply for the marriage license.

At one point, Mengele had problems with the Buenos Aires police, who suspected that he was practicing medicine without a license. What led them to this suspicion is unknown, and it frightened Mengele. Leaving Martha and her son in Buenos Aires, Mengele decided to flee to Paraguay. A person could disappear in

WANTED

Dr. Josef Mengele
For his crimes against humanity

Josef Mengele was responsible for the death of 400,000 persons at Auschwitz Concentration Camp. He tortured children and made their parents suffer. He brutalized people with horrible medical experiments.

Mengele is 74. Height 1.7 m (5'10"). Eyes, greenish brown. He became a citizen of Argentina in 1954, a citizen of Paraguay in 1959.

Rewards worldwide total more than U.S. $2.375 million for information leading to the arrest and extradition of Dr. Josef Mengele.

Contact: Martin Mendelsohn, P.O. Box 33126, Washington, D.C. 20033, or call Simon Wiesenthal Center, (213) 553-9036. All information will be held confidential.

Dr. Mengele in his mid 40's.

An artist conception of what Mengele would look like today at age 74.

REWARDS–U.S. $2,375,000

Despite the large reward offered for his capture, Mengele managed to live on the run in South America until his death in 1979.

Paraguay, which is why he chose it. Martha and her son made regular visits to his new home there.

Over the next several years, Mengele managed to stay free. Through the efforts of those who were determined to see justice done, it became known that Mengele was alive and living on the run in South America. Multiple governments failed in attempts to have Mengele captured. Those who visited him in his new life never disclosed his whereabouts. The Mengele family photo album has photos of Mengele well into his later years.

Getting Away with Murder

Dr. Mengele was charged with crimes against humanity, including selections (*Selektionen*), lethal phenol injections, beatings, shootings, and other forms of deliberate killing. He was never tried for those crimes. Whether he ever experienced true remorse for his hideous behavior will never be known. What is known is that Mengele was a product of his culture and times. Germany and its circumstances helped to shape the man who came to be known as the Angel of Death. Instead of being hanged like his Nazi colleagues, Mengele spent the rest of his life on borrowed time.

It is believed that in February of 1979, Mengele drowned in the waters off Bertioga, Brazil. Friends of Mengele brought his body back to the beach after seeing him struggle in the surf. His death was kept a secret by family and friends. The bones were finally autopsied by authorities in 1985 and declared to be Josef Mengele's.

Today, the Mengele family continues to run the foundry in Günzburg. There are memorials and a street in the town dedicated to Karl, Mengele's father. Ironically, Mengele—who set out to find fame despite his family's success—is not memorialized in his birthplace. He is the purposely forgotten member of the Mengele family.

Timeline

March 1911	Josef Mengele is born in Germany.
1914–1918	Germany participates in World War I under the leadership of the Kaiser.
1919–1933	Germany has a democratic government, a period known as the Weimar Republic.
1924	Hitler writes *Mein Kampf.*
October 1930	Mengele begins classes at Munich University.
August 1934	Hitler proclaims himself Führer.
September 1935	Anti-Semitic laws are enacted.
1938	Mengele receives his license to practice medicine from the University of Frankfurt.

November 1938	*Kristallnacht.*
September 1939	Germany invades Poland.
May 1940	Auschwitz opens.
1940–1942	Mengele serves in the SS.
June 1941	Germany invades the Soviet Union.
July 1941	The Final Solution begins.
May 1943	Mengele is stationed at Auschwitz.
June 1944	Allies mount a massive attack against Germany.
January 1945	Mengele's flight from justice begins.
April 1945	Hitler commits suicide.
May 1945	Germany surrenders.
August 1949	Mengele flees to South America.
February 1979	Mengele drowns while swimming with friends.
June 1985	The bones of a body in South America are identified as Mengele's.

Glossary

Allies
Great Britain, the United States, the Soviet Union, and other nations that went to war against Nazi Germany and its allies, which were known as the Axis powers.

anti-Semitism
Prejudice or discrimination against people of the Jewish religion.

Aryan
The Nazis used this term to describe people of Northern European descent, usually with blond hair and blue eyes.

Aryanization
The taking over of Jewish jobs and businesses by non-Jewish German people.

asocials
People deemed unworthy by Nazis, such as
   Gypsies, homosexuals, and the mentally and
   physically disabled.

Auschwitz
The largest Nazi concentration and death camp,
   located in Poland.

concentration camps
Prison camps built to hold Jews, political
   prisoners, and asocials.

death camp
Camp where mass numbers of people were killed.

Einsatzgruppen
Mobile killing units of the SS.

eugenics
A science that focuses on improving hereditary
   qualities of a race, usually by control of
   human mating.

Final Solution
A plan for the complete destruction of European
   Jews.

Führer
A German word meaning *leader*.

Lebensraum
A Nazi term meaning *living space*.

Mischlinge
A Nazi term for people of mixed German and
Jewish ancestry.

Nazi
An abbreviation for the National Socialist German
Workers Party.

occupation
When a country at war takes over an area of
another country or territory.

propaganda
The spreading of ideas, misinformation, and
rumors for the purpose of helping a cause.

SA—*Sturmabteilung*
A Nazi military branch, also known as Storm
Troopers or Brown Shirts.

SS—*Schutzstaffel*
A large Nazi military group, also known as the
　　Protection Squad.

Selektionen
The Nazi system of separating prisoners and
　　deciding who was to live and who was to die.

Stahlhelm
The Steel Helmets, a nationalistic, anti-
　　Semitic group.

Third Reich
The Nazi German Empire.

Weimar Republic
German government established after World War I,
　　which governed from 1919-1933.

For More Information

CANDLES Holocaust Museum
1532 South Third Street
Terre Haute, IN 47802
(812) 234-7881
Web site: http://candles-museum.com
CANDLES educates the public about the Holocaust with
    firsthand experiences of survivors.

Simon Wiesenthal Center
1399 South Roxbury
Los Angeles, CA 90035
(310) 553-9036
(800) 900-9036
http://www.wiesenthal.org

In Canada

Friends of Simon Wiesenthal Center for
    Holocaust Studies
8 King Street East, Suite 1300

Toronto, ON M5C 1B5
(416) 864-9735

Veterans Affairs Canada
http://www.vac-acc.gc.ca/
    general/sub.cfm?source=history/secondwar
Collection of information on the Canadian
    experience of WWII.

Videography

The Holocaust—In Memory of Millions (1993).

Night and Fog (1995).

Survivors of the Holocaust (1995).

Survivors (CD-ROM) (1999).

Web Sites

Auschwitz Alphabet
http://www.spectacle.org/695/ausch.html

The Holocaust Chronicle
http://www.holocaustchronicle.org/HC_Start.html

Museum of Tolerance Simon Wiesenthal Center
http://wiesenthal.com/mot/index.cfm

United States Holocaust Memorial Museum
http://www.ushmm.org

For Further Reading

Frank, Anne. *Diary of a Young Girl: The Definitive Edition.* New York: Bantam Books, 1997.

Grossman, Mendel (photographer), and Frank Dabba Smith. *My Secret Camera: Life in the Lodz Ghetto.* San Diego, CA: Gulliver Books, 2000.

Hogan, David J, ed. *The Holocaust Chronicle.* Lincolnwood, IL: Louis Webber Publications International, Ltd, 2000.

Leapman, Michael. *Witnesses to War: Eight True-Life Stories of Nazi Persecution.* New York: Puffin-Penguin Putnam, Inc., 2000.

Warren, Andrea. *Surviving Hitler: A Boy in the Nazi Death Camps.* New York: HarperCollins Children's Books, 2001.

For Advanced Readers

Lifton, Robert Jay. *The Nazi Doctors.* 2nd ed. New York: Basic Books, 2000.

Posner, Gerald L., and John Ware. *Mengele: The Complete Story.* 2nd Ed. New York: Cooper Square Press, 2000.

Index

Credits

About the author
Holly Cefrey is a freelance writer and researcher.

Photo Credits
Cover © Archive Photos; p. 4 map by Martin Gilbert, *Atlas of the Holocaust*, William Morrow, New York, revised edition, 1993; p. 8 © Lydia Chagoll, courtesy of United States Holocaust Memorial Musuem (USHMM) Photo Archives; pp. 10, 40, 55 © National Archives, courtesy of USHMM Photo Archives; p. 17 © Popperfoto/Archive Photos; p. 18 © Virginius Dabney, courtesy of USHMM Photo Archives; p. 24 © Owen Franken/

Series Design
Cynthia Williamson